Personality Mis-Profiles

Have you been stereotyped?

Henry W. Wright

HENRY W. WRIGHT

4178 Crest Highway
Thomaston, Georgia 30286

www.beinhealth.com

EAN: 978-1-934680-14-8

Copyright Notice

© Copyright: 2007. Be in Health™

All rights reserved. Any material, be it in written form, audio, video, compact disc, website postings – whether it be text, HTML, audio streaming or graphic images related to Be in Health™ may not be mirrored, reproduced, or displayed in whole or in part on another webpage or website (whatever the nature or purpose), or in any publication or collection of widespread circulation, whether offline or online (whatever the nature or purpose), even if considered "fair use," without express written permission from Be in Health™.

Disclaimer

This ministry does not seek to be in conflict with any medical or psychiatric practices nor do we seek to be in conflict with any church and its religious doctrines, beliefs or practices. We are not a part of medicine or psychology, yet we work to make them more effective, rather than working against them. We believe many human problems are fundamentally spiritual with associated physiological and psychological manifestations. This information is intended for your general knowledge only. Information is presented only to give insight into disease, its problems and its possible solutions in the area of disease eradication and/or prevention. It is not a substitute for medical advice or treatment for specific medical conditions or disorders. You should seek prompt medical care for any specific health issues. Treatment modalities around your specific health issues are between you and your physician.

We are not responsible for a person's disease, nor are we responsible for his/her healing. All we can do is share what we see about a problem. We are not professionals; we are not healers. We are administering the Scriptures, and what they say about this subject, along with what the medical and scientific communities have also observed in line with this insight. There is no guarantee that any person will be healed or any disease be prevented. The fruits of this teaching will come forth out of the relationship between the person and God based on these insights given and applied. This ministry is patterned after the following scriptures: 2 Corinthians 5:18-20; 1 Corinthians 12; Ephesians 4; Mark 16:15-20.

Preface

This booklet was developed from a teaching to a live audience and has been kept in a conversational format. It is designed to reach a personal level with the reader rather than present a structured, theological presentation. Many times the reader will feel that Henry Wright is talking directly to him or her. The frequent use of the pronoun *you* is meant to penetrate the human heart for conviction, not for accusation.

Table of Contents

Introduction 1
   Examples of Profiles 2
     Astrology 2
     Disease Labels in Allopathic Medicine 6
Autoimmune Disease in the Church 9
Law of Sin 13
   Sin is a Being 15
   Jungian Psychology 15
Three Stages of Freedom 19
   Stage One: Knowledge 19
     The Tools for Victory 20
     Antidote to the Lies 21
     All Error is Insane 22
   Stage Two: Spiritual Warfare 23
     Shadowboxing 25
   Stage Three: Deliverance 26
Sanctification 27
   Timed Release in Sanctification 27
   Lies vs. Truth 30
Fabricated Personalities 35
   Personalities by Nature 39
   Mind/Body Connection 41
     Serotonin 42
   Motive of the Heart 44

    Dead Works vs. Fruit of the Spirit 45
Doctrines of Christ 47
    Repentance From Dead Works 48
        Dead Works 51
        Apply the Word Daily 56
        Righteousness Represents the Father 58
        Peace Comes from Jesus the WORD 58
        Fellowship with the Godhead 59
        The Blessings of Obedience 60
        The Enemy and Timed Release 60
    Black and White 61
        A Lighter Gray 61
Our Relationship with Others 62
    The Role of Pastor 63
        The Church and Healing of the Body 64
        Fear of Man 64
        Fear of Rejection 65
        Fear of Failure 65
        Fear of Abandonment 65
Conclusion 70

Now the Lord is that Spirit:
and where the Spirit of the Lord is,
there is liberty. But we all, with
open face beholding as in a glass the
glory of the Lord,
are changed into the same image
from glory to glory,
even as by the Spirit of the Lord.

2 Corinthians 3:17-18

Personality Mis-Profiles

Introduction

One of the goals I hope to achieve in the ministry of healing is to give you back to God the way He saw you from the foundation of the world. I believe God has a perfect will from the foundation of the world for everyone and He, through the Holy Spirit, desires to develop and lead you to be the man or woman He saw from the foundation of the world.

What I see happening in the world today is God's people are bound to an identity or label. The Christian church is filled with seminars, often organized and run by their pastors, elders or deacons who are trying to help the members understand themselves and each other by their personality type. That binds them to a label. They are being asked to conform to an image.

You need to be released from all modalities of psychological and spiritual profiling. That does not mean just from leaders and teachers, but also from parents and friends and anyone else that has labeled you. You may have labeled yourself. You must be released from all of that because it eliminates the work of the Holy Spirit.

When I was meditating on this subject, I knew I would probably bump into some of your sacred cows. If I do I will just have to ask you to kill them. Have a barbeque because old wives' tales and fables, doctrines of devils, humanistic precepts, psychological modalities and profiles do a wonderful job of showing us who we *are not* in Christ. They have done a wonderful job of establishing us in our breakdown.

EXAMPLES OF PROFILES

Astrology

Someone came to me who had been saved and healed for a few years, but was still into astrology. This person was filled with the Holy Ghost and water baptized, but had not fallen out of agreement with astrology. She firmly believed that the whole system of astrology identified the present and future for us. She had been trying to help people identify with the sun, moon and stars in the fourteenth quadrant of the seventh cusp of whatever.

Anyway this person came into my office ready to debate with me and to make me a disciple of astrology. When she came in, I sat back and listened. I finally said, "I don't doubt the fact that you really want to help people. I believe you are sincere, but I have difficulty with something." She asked what that was.

I said, "When you go to astrology, you are identifying who you are in creation according to your precepts and your modalities of thinking of what is in the sun, moon, stars and the whole nine yards. That's going to be your day. That's going to be who you are.

Personality Mis-Profiles

"If you have the characteristics of a Leo, or a Libra or a Sagittarius or whatever it is, that's who you are. Everything that is going to happen to you in the future rotates around this pre-determined aspect of your nature and existence.

"In astrology there's no changing into His image. If you have a defect in your nature, you're stuck with it and you're going to have a bad day. You had better be prepared for it because it's coming, and there's nothing you can do. And if you're going to have a blessed day, there's nothing you can do about that either. It's in the stars. You're preaching a gospel of fatalistic thinking."

All of a sudden the lights came on for this person and she said, "I can't bind people to what is. You're right, Pastor. Astrology binds people to what they are and what will happen tomorrow. I mean, look what God's done for me already. I was stuck in that stuff and now I'm changed."

Instantly, years and years of a mindset disappeared. Actually it did not disappear; it became inferior to a superior way of thinking. That is the mind of Christ.

Every label that someone has put on you is a form of astrology. It is time to trash those labels!

We had someone here who was a pastor of a church. He went back home and attended a seminar for pastors in his denomination. In their teaching they outlined psychological profiles for pastoral leadership. It was said the proper or preferred type of man to be set in leadership should be an extrovert because introverted people would naturally follow extroverts.

During the course of this seminar they did psychological profiles on their own ministers. When they were finished they determined that this person should be an assistant pastor or a deacon and another person should be the leader.

There is no scriptural basis that makes being an extrovert criterion for being a leader of God's people. In fact, many of God's greatest leaders were introverts. The pastor I am talking about is an existing pastor who has been told that, because he meets the classification of an introvert, it would be better for him to be reclassified as an assistant pastor or a deacon. He was told he should be removed from his pastoral duties.

Who called this man anyway? Who calls a man to ministry—the denomination or God? Who is the man responding to? A psychological profile!

God uses weak vessels to turn the world upside down. The Word says the 12 disciples were ignorant and unlearned men who turned the world upside down.

> **Now when they saw the boldness of Peter and John, and perceived that they were unlearned and ignorant men, they marvelled; and they took knowledge of them, that they had been with Jesus.** Acts 4:13

Moses was an introvert. Jeremiah said, "Who am I? I'm a child. Why choose me?"

Isaiah said, "I'm a man of unclean lips." What about little David? He was on the backside of the sheepfold. He was doing the lowliest of all duties. There was no occupation in those days with a lower status or rank than tending sheep.

Jesus was a Lamb led to the slaughter. Isaiah pictured Him in physique as one who was not comely.

Personality Mis-Profiles

You would not have any desire of Him as a man, yet we make pictures of an effeminate man with long hair and beautiful brown eyes that stands about 6 foot 5 and call him Jesus. The Word does not give a picture of what Jesus looks like, but Isaiah says He was uncomely.

> For he shall grow up before him as a tender plant, and as a root out of a dry ground: he hath no form nor comeliness; and when we shall see him, *there is* no beauty that we should desire him.   Isaiah 53:2

What happens when someone labels you with something positive and then you start to conform to that image? If you study or participate in certain circles of the modern day prophetic movement, you get it full blast. If you want to be perfect and good in Christ, just get around these circles. They teach only good things are going to happen. What comes out of that is, "Oh, he's a good one, isn't he?" Too often there is no regard to sanctification because people just strive to work it out in the flesh.

I am not against prophesying; do not misunderstand me. I am against counterfeiting the real thing. This is a touchy issue because the prophetic movement is big in America. Too often people are given a word, a profile about themselves and/or a prophecy or word about their future. They are told who they will be, how perfect they will be, what kind of ministry they will have. They are even told what kind of Christian or believer they will be.

Because it is not a finished product, they will attempt to become that prophecy in the flesh because it is expected of them. As they attempt to become that prophecy or word, they go right down under it. These improperly instructed believers are sick because they are driven to conform to something that is not a work of the Holy Spirit. It is the work of another kingdom.

Disease Labels in Allopathic Medicine

In the diagnosis of disease from the allopathic standpoint, all you have is what the devil has done to the human body. You have an observation, a definition and an identification of the breakdown in creation. Then we call it incurable or inevitable. That represents another doctrine that is fatalistic in its intent.

You may have a disease but you are not a disease

You may have a disease, but you are not a disease. The enemy wants you to become one with disease. He wants your nature—body, soul, and spirit—to be identified with something other than what God created. The enemy wants others to come along and label you in it so you can be conformed to this image the rest of your days.

I do not think Jesus agreed with the labeling placed on the Gadarene demoniac. The only thing that separated that man from what God created him to be from the foundation of the world was a spirit of insanity. In fact, Jesus called it an unclean spirit, and later the thing identified itself as Legion: "We are many." That is the record of Scripture.

The tormented man described in Mark 5 and Luke 8 was supposed to be in his right mind living at peace

Personality Mis-Profiles

with his family. When it was over, he went back with a sound mind to live with his family. Do you think his local community labeled him? Most likely they did. After all, someone living in the tombs, running around naked, screaming at the top of his lungs and cutting himself would have been enough to get him labeled.

You might as well fall out of agreement with stereotyping and profiling. I am just a short little guy, average for the planet. One day we were at our favorite restaurant and they had a new manager. This guy looked like he should be the president of a large corporation. He was like Saul.

> ¹Now there was a man of Benjamin, whose name was Kish, the son of Abiel, the son of Zeror, the son of Bechorath, the son of Aphiah, a Benjamite, a mighty man of power.
> ²And he had a son, whose name was Saul, a choice young man, and a goodly: and there was not among the children of Israel a goodlier person than he: from his shoulders and upward *he* was higher than any of the people.
> 1 Samuel 9:1-2

This new manager had to be 6 foot 7. He was head and shoulders above the rest. He carried about his managerial duties as if he were gliding on ice like a figure skater. He captured my attention. He looked like a man you could follow in the restaurant industry.

All of a sudden, I started to compare myself to him. Guess who was on my shoulder? I had something comparing me to me, and using him as an example of comparison. I finally looked at my wife and said. "Look at that guy. Wouldn't he make a good pastor? Can't you

7

just see him with the sheep? He'd be head and shoulders above them. I mean just look at him!"

My wife and my daughter looked at me and laughed. They said, "Who are you listening to? Where are you coming from? Do you think we'd follow him? He's not a sheep herder. His head's too high in the clouds. We wouldn't follow him. We have a sheepherder: it's you."

They did not cut me any slack. They continued, "What you're looking at, we wouldn't follow."

I said, "Really?" They were not nice about it. They took my discernment and trashed it.

My desire is to release you back into the kingdom of God without all these sacred cows hanging around your neck accusing you and tearing you down. The biggest problem we have in Rejection is comparing ourselves to another.

Why would you compare yourself to another anyway? They did not create you. God did. They did not call you. They did not save you. They did not anoint you. They are not going to raise you from the dead. They are not going to redeem you. They are not going to deliver you. They are not going to heal you.

Paul said,

> Be ye followers of me, even as I also *am* of Christ.   1 Corinthians 11:1

Do not be a clone of some other human image, no matter how spiritual they are. I am not your standard and neither is anyone else. If you followed some of Paul's sin that lived in him, you would be in trouble.

Romans 7 is refreshing because it gives you the ability to be in relationship with God in your calling and anointing and whoever you are, and still be dealing with your stuff.

Any type of caste system, whether it is inside or outside of the church, is absolute heresy.

The Word of God says,

> There is neither Jew nor Greek, there is neither bond nor free, there is neither male nor female: for ye are all one in Christ Jesus.
> Galatians 3:28

Autoimmune Disease in the Church

I think sometimes the Christian church is known more for killing its wounded than anything else. It is amazing how we want to evangelize the world but kill each other. We judge each other after the flesh, binding each other to our un-renewed parts. Or perhaps we do not allow the Holy Spirit to truly lead someone into who He has made them to be.

I am fully convinced the body of Christ has an autoimmune disease. In an autoimmune disease, your own body will destroy its own flesh and tissue. Sometimes in the body of Christ, we damage each other with labels, stigmas and stereotypes.

In many churches, whoever you are when you come into the church usually is who you are the rest of your duration in that church. If you were a bum that was saved, you certainly will not be asked to be a member of the church board. Everything that happens around church organization is assigned to those who are born righteous, those who came in "clean" without a problem. If you do not have the right background and speak the right lingo, you are not spiritual.

I cannot bind you to what is not of God. I cannot make you one with evil. I need to make provision for you in it because that is the work of sanctification. I am able to separate you from your evil and sin. Can you separate yourself from it?

I had a '57 Chevy convertible several years ago. It was beautiful. It had yellow and black pleated leather interior, a black top, oversized tires with mag wheels and black beauty mufflers. I bought it for $3,300.

After about three years, old paint and rust from the previous owner was starting to show. I took it to a place that fixes stuff like that. They looked at the car and said, "We have to strip the car back to the frame. Disassemble it and start from scratch. No bondo. All new metal. Sandblast the frame."

I said, "How much?"

He said, "$13,000."

I tacked $13,000 to $3,300 and said, "OUCH!" If I did not do it, the car would be worthless. So I got rid of the car. I just figured it was one of those idols anyway. Today, if I had put $13,000 into it, that car would be worth over $50,000.

Sometimes we dress up in righteousness because it is expected of us. Because there is a caste system in the Christian church and in most other sectors in the world, we cannot be transparent with our rust. So when our rust starts showing, we run down to the body shop and ask for a quick spray job.

If we acknowledge we have rust then we are judged according to our rust, not according to what the manufacturer designed from the beginning which can be restored. We are worth the $13,000 restoration! When we are finished, instead of being on the junk heap, we will be worth a small fortune in our restored state for both God and mankind. It is a good investment. You do not have to settle for a cheaper model like I did. The investment is worth it.

> **And he said unto me, My grace is sufficient for thee: for my strength is made perfect in weakness. Most gladly therefore will I rather glory in my infirmities, that the power of Christ may rest upon me.** 2 Corinthians 12:9

So what if you do not have it all together? Paul didn't. Moses certainly did not have it together either. He was a murderer. In today's church he would be considered a social psychopath. Jeremiah did not have it together. One minute he said, "Oh, there's a fire that burns within me, it cannot be quenched." Two breaths later, "I curse the day my mother ever had me."

You are struggling with stuff coming out of your generations. You are being asked to conform to the image of the god of this world and to the image of the generational curses of your ancestry, along with humanistic profiles that have nothing to do with who God created.

Many people will not be healed until these labels are stripped off; they have become one with what the devil has done to their lives. When God did the work of creation in Genesis, He did not say it was good, He said it was "very" good.

Jeremiah reads,

> ⁴Then the word of the Lord came unto me, saying,
> ⁵Before I formed thee in the belly I knew thee; and before thou camest forth out of the womb I sanctified thee, and I ordained thee a prophet unto the nations. Jeremiah 1:4-5

After hearing this great revelation from God, Jeremiah immediately went into lack of self-esteem. He lined up not with what God thought, but with what he thought according to the inherited evil spirits of his ancestry. Do you think he had a lack of self-confidence? He said, "Oh Lord God, behold I cannot speak for I'm a child."

> Then said I, Ah, Lord GOD! behold, I cannot speak: for I *am* a child. Jeremiah 1:6

Look at the Lord's response:

> ⁷But the Lord said unto me, Say not, I *am* a child: for thou shalt go to all that I shall send thee, and whatsoever I command thee thou shalt speak.
> ⁸Be not afraid of their faces: for I *am* with thee to deliver thee, saith the Lord. Jeremiah 1:7-8

Do you think Jeremiah might have had Fear[1] of man? Possibly so.

---

[1] Fear and the names of other entities in the kingdom of darkness are capitalized.

If you bind yourself to the personality of sin to any degree, then you have bound yourself to it of your own free will. I want to bring you to a place to encourage you because when you are faced with what you are not, that is all you can see. I would not be in ministry if I could not see you as God saw you from the foundation of the world. I would stumble over you, and you would probably stumble over me. We would go nowhere.

Law of Sin

Paul taught in Romans 7 that the law establishes the knowledge of good and evil.

> **If then I do that which I would not, I consent unto the law that *it is* good.** Romans 7:16

When I do evil, I am calling the Word of God evil, and calling the new law I have established good. Have you ever found y yourself walking there? If the Word tells you to forgive your neighbor and you do not, you are calling the law of God evil and this new law of unforgiveness good.

> **Now then it is no more I that do it, but sin that dwelleth in me.** Romans 7:17

It is not even Paul doing the things that he hates! Why would you want to become one with things that are not of God, when it is not you doing it anyway? You say, "But it is me doing it." Well if you participate with it, then that certainly will become your sin.

In the initial stages of whatever modality you are following, it is not you doing it. It is the sin that dwells in you. Even after the sin has taken root, it still is not the real you acting out the sin. You are participating with it and are therefore guilty, but the *sin is not you.*

> [18]For I know that in me (that is, in my flesh,) dwelleth no good thing: for to will is present with me; but *how* to perform that which is good I find not.
> [19]For the good that I would I do not: but the evil which I would not, that I do.
> [20]Now if I do that I would not, it is no more I that do it, but sin that dwelleth in me.
> Romans 7:18-20

This sin that dwelt in Paul is what Jungian psychology has termed archetypes and dark shadows.

> [20]Now if I do that I would not, it is no more I that do it, but sin that dwelleth in me.
> [21]I find then a law, that, when I would do good, evil is present with me.
> [22]For I delight in the law of God after the inward man:
> [23]But I see another law in my members, warring against the law of my mind, and bringing me into captivity to the law of sin which is in my members.
> [24]O wretched man that I am! who shall deliver me from the body of this death?
> [25]I thank God through Jesus Christ our Lord. So then with the mind I myself serve the law of God; but with the flesh the law of sin.
> Romans 7:20-25

Here is the battleground: "So then with the mind I myself serve the law of God; but with the flesh the law of sin."

SIN IS A BEING

I have taken a firm position in ministry that sin is a being. "Through one man sin entered into the world." When we partake with the being of sin it becomes our sin in participation. We need to repent and deal with it.

If something has attached itself to me and it is neither my heart nor part of my creation from the foundation of the world, then I am able to divest myself of it. Before God, I put it on notice and separate myself from it in my thinking. I can then be renewed and delivered. I do not have to be one with indwelling sin.

JUNGIAN PSYCHOLOGY

Psychology has proposed various methods or coping tools to "handle" this common struggle of indwelling sin. Karl Jung, the son of a German protestant pastor, watched his father minister to his congregation with no insight or solution into their mental problems or biological diseases. He purposed in his heart to create an alternative to Christianity, because he perceived Christianity was a dead religion. He eventually developed what is known today as Jungian psychology.

In his theory, Jung hypothesized a dualistic compartment of the soul consisting of the conscious and the collective unconscious. He also taught archetypes and dark shadows are the inherited historical darkness of your family tree residing in your collective unconscious. In his writings, he states it all came to him through the channeling of a spirit called "Philemon."

I consider Karl Jung's theory to be heresy. Psychology is a form of insanity that identifies the works of the devil and establishes them. This is no different than allopathic medicine. The Bible does not teach about the collective unconscious; it is not a scriptural precept. What Karl Jung calls the collective unconscious is, in fact, the spirit of man. These so-called archetypes and dark shadows dwell within the spirit of man. I believe this is indwelling sin.

Karl Jung's intent was to make a scientific statement to a pagan world. He knew they would not believe what Scripture has to say about evil spirits. He changed the name of devils and evil spirits to archetypes and dark shadows to accommodate a scientific world. He also changed the spirit realm into the collective unconscious, which contrasts the truth outlined in Hebrews.

> **For the word of God *is* quick, and powerful, and sharper than any twoedged sword, piercing even to the dividing asunder of soul and spirit, and of the joints and marrow, and *is* a discerner of the thoughts and intents of the heart.**
>
> Hebrews 4:12

Today in psychotherapy, you are taught to come into contact with the archetypes and dark shadows of your collective unconscious to identify the vestiges of your ancestral darkness. Once those archetypes are identified, you are then more aware of your breakdown and can then cohabit with them according to knowledge.

They believe you are equipped to have a better day because you understand the dark part of you that is tormenting you. At least you know about it. You are counseled or taught how to work with it. Often this type of counsel involves blocking your reality through drugs. Do you think that is the gospel of our God?

Our Creator ought to be able to fix our problems. He is the One that made us and knew us from the beginning. I believe God is able to fix us on all three levels: spirit, soul and body.

> **And the very God of peace sanctify you wholly; and *I pray God* your whole spirit and soul and body be preserved blameless unto the coming of our Lord Jesus Christ.**
> 1 Thessalonians 5:23

Let's say your name is Oscar and you live in a trash can. You have been given a personality profile that says that you are grouchy. So you come out of the trash can grouchy. In order to meet you, we are going to brand you.

You are a lovely saint, but you are a grouch. We are going to accommodate you and make you part of us as the body of Christ, but we are going to have to include the aspect of your nature that is grouchy. That is your name, after all! Then we will flow together in one body and spirit.

If you were a grouch, then because I love you I would accommodate you. But I could not accept that for you as a way of life forever. It would not meet the nature of God because God is not a grouch. We have been created in His image, and from glory to glory we are being changed into His image. The mind of Christ is not being a grouch. When this aspect of your personality, being a grouch, manifests, it would not be you; it would be your sin nature. It would be indwelling sin. I could not call you Oscar.

We have had this mentality that because we are born again we are sanctified. We have been taught we are already sanctified; we just have not appropriated it. To a degree that is true, but it really is not that way. Do we appropriate sanctification? Or is it a matter of killing something that is in us that should not be there?

Freedom still requires responsibility.

> **And having in a readiness to revenge all disobedience, when your obedience is fulfilled.**
> 2 Corinthians 10:6

The church has been taught much about promise but not about discernment, so we are still in bondage. We have been taught righteousness, but making righteousness part of our heart is another matter. I firmly believe the next move of God on the earth and in this nation will be a move of sanctification. Then we will see God's power unleashed and unchecked, "Having in a readiness to revenge all disobedience when your obedience is fulfilled."

When sanctification is taught, many times it is taught from a legalistic standpoint of performance. This produces more condemnation, guilt and shame because if your heart is not in it, you become a hypocrite.

I teach sanctification and righteousness as tight as anyone teaches it in America, but I do not use it as a weapon to oppress you. I do not use it to force you into works of righteousness. I do not judge you. When you do not do works of righteousness, I do not judge you according to it.

I am not the judge; I am just the guy serving. The judge is on the throne and He will judge. So if I am serving, I cannot force you to do anything. God, who is greatest of all, has never forced me to do anything. So if God has never forced me to anything in righteousness, why should I as a minister force you?

Can I do anything more for you than you are already allowing God to do in your life? If I tried, I would be getting ahead of God. I would be doing it out of my knowledge, my understanding of the Word, my gifts or my anointing. Just because I see what you should be like and the battleground, and the darkness that should growing light, it does not mean a thing. All I can do is lead you to the place where God the Holy Spirit can perfect this in your life.

If I try to lead you past where you are now without your agreement, then I have superseded the living God. Then I have become a god to you and He is not going to put up with it. If you are not listening to Him, why should you listen to me? Do not obey me and use me as the standard. I am just a servant.

I will teach you sanctification and righteousness and holiness. I will teach it to you because if I do not, I cannot get the curse broken.

Three Stages of Freedom

STAGE ONE: KNOWLEDGE

The first stage to freedom is knowledge. Let's look at the scriptures:

> So then faith *cometh* by hearing, and hearing by the word of God.　　　　　Romans 10:17
>
> And ye shall know the truth, and the truth shall make you free.　　　　　John 8:32
>
> Therefore my people are gone into captivity, because *they have* no knowledge: and their honourable men *are* famished, and their multitude dried up with thirst.　　　Isaiah 5:13
>
> My people are destroyed for lack of knowledge: because thou hast rejected knowledge, I will also reject thee, that thou shalt be no priest to me: seeing thou hast forgotten the law of thy God, I will also forget thy children.
> 　　　　　Hosea 4:6

Knowledge gives you discernment.

Paul said,

> Therefore by the deeds of the law there shall no flesh be justified in his sight: for by the law *is* the knowledge of sin.　　　　　Romans 3:20

The Tools for Victory

The Word of God will give you the tools for walking in freedom and victory. The Scriptures tell us God is love and He loves you. "If God be for you, who can be against you?" We can quote many scriptures telling us God loves us, even if we still have sin in our lives. You need to mix it with your faith. Take the lie in your mind and cast it down as a lying imagination because it does not match the knowledge of God. You say it is so hard when your mind is filled with these thoughts! It is time for the antidote.

Antidote to the Lies

What is the antidote? It is the mind of Christ; the Word of God. Who are you going to believe? Whose report are you going to believe?

Will you believe old programming or what God says? I think it is time to come out of agreement with the devil. I do not mean him personally. It is time for you to come out of agreement with the lies. He is and was the father of all lies. If he can get you to believe a lie, then your spirit, soul and body will conform to that image.

> So shall they fear the name of the LORD from the west, and his glory from the rising of the sun. When the enemy shall come in like a flood, the Spirit of the LORD shall lift up a standard against him. Isaiah 59:19

> ¹²For the word of God *is* quick, and powerful, and sharper than any twoedged sword, piercing even to the dividing asunder of soul and spirit, and of the joints and marrow, and *is* a discerner of the thoughts and intents of the heart.
> ¹³Neither is there any creature that is not manifest in his sight: but all things *are* naked and opened unto the eyes of him with whom we have to do. Hebrews 4:12-13

The Word of God discerns our thoughts. At any given moment our thoughts can be from ourselves, the enemy or God. If Satan can appear as an angel of light, he can appear *as you* to yourself. He can convince you the garbage you have running in your mind is you. He can speak in your voice and convince you *he is you*.

The only sanity that we have in regards to our thoughts is to know what God has to say about a subject.

We can get caught in our minds with precepts, concepts, thoughts and realities that do not match the Word.

All Error is Insane

All error is a form of insanity. Insanity is when your thoughts do not match reality. Your thoughts and your truth are not truth. Many false religions are based on faulty precepts filled with divination and error. That is a form of insanity.

If you have ever had Self-hatred, Rejection and/or Guilt, those thoughts and memories from the past will be there. I can go back to my days of sin. I can go back to my days of depression. I can go back to my days of fear. I can do it right now. I can remember those days, but I have subjected that reality to a higher reality.

Those thoughts are now inferior because my being is lined up with what the Word of God says about me, not what others or the enemy may have told me. Yes, sometimes I do have thoughts of Unloving, Guilt, Self-hatred, Fear and Rejection. Those spirits will stalk us all the days of our lives, but we do not have to open the door when they come knocking.

Hebrews says,

> **But strong meat belongeth to them that are of full age, even those who by reason of use have their senses exercised to discern both good and evil.**　　　　　　　　　Hebrews 5:14

This is a pragmatic application, day by day, of discerning both good and evil. This is not sin consciousness. This discernment *separates* you from sin. The Word of God anointed by the Holy Spirit brings you to spiritual understanding. Your mind is renewed continually by revelation until it is cleansed of evil thoughts and realities.

As a son of God, the Spirit of God is within me to lead me into all truth. By obtaining knowledge there can be objectivity in bondage preceding freedom. It is possible to be free and not be free. You can still be in bondage, but walk in freedom. You cannot be free unless you understand what the freedom represents. The worst thing I could do is to cast out an evil spirit without laying a foundation of knowledge.

If someone has an evil entity, we must fill them up with God's truth and knowledge until that evil spirit is literally squeezed out. We want to bring them to a place where there is no room for it anymore.

Paul taught that "sin" is not our identity. But the enemy will attempt to obscure our real identity in Christ by holding up his flash card accusing us of who he is in our lives. We can defeat him by applying the Word in discernment. The Bible says that we are to be wiser than a serpent and harmless as a dove. What does it mean to be wiser than a serpent? It means if we have the Word of God and the mind of Christ, we can think better than Satan does.

STAGE TWO: SPIRITUAL WARFARE

The second stage is to Resist the devil, and he shall flee.

> [7]Submit yourselves therefore to God. Resist the devil, and he will flee from you.

> [8]Draw nigh to God, and he will draw nigh to you. Cleanse *your* hands, *ye* sinners; and purify *your* hearts, *ye* double-minded.　　James 4:7-8

What comes first? Submit to God. The Word says your sins have separated you from your God. If you are going to submit to God, what is the first thing you do? You build an altar of sanctification. Then you bring yourself as a living sacrifice. You lay it right down. You are going to crucify the flesh and you might as well prepare to die. Something has to die! Putting to death whatever is not of God will cause you to live.

I quit going to spiritual warfare conferences about 10 years ago. I quit reading books and listening to tapes on spiritual warfare because every bit of it was shadow boxing. It was designed around an invisible enemy called Satan. They were not teaching the real battleground.

The devil is not omnipresent or omniscient. He does not understand all things. He walks invisibly up and down in the earth.

> [6]Now there was a day when the sons of God came to present themselves before the LORD, and Satan came also among them.
> [7]And the LORD said unto Satan, Whence comest thou? Then Satan answered the LORD, and said, From going to and fro in the earth, and from walking up and down in it.　　Job 1:6-7

Satan administers an invisible kingdom. When you resist the devil, you are really resisting his kingdom of principalities, powers, spiritual wickedness in high places and the rulers of darkness.

Shadowboxing

You might as well get a good picture of him before you defeat him. No shadowboxing here! You need to know who you are resisting, why you are resisting him, how he got there and why he needs to not be there.

You are resisting thoughts of evil such as Doubt and Unbelief, Guilt and Self-hatred. If the Word says God has not given you a spirit of Fear and you find it in your life, then you do warfare against the spirit of Fear.

> **For God hath not given us the spirit of fear; but of power, and of love, and of a sound mind.**
> 2 Timothy 1:7

The Bible says,

> **What shall we then say to these things? If God** *be* **for us, who** *can be* **against us?** Romans 8:31

When you have thoughts that accuse God and tear down who you are in Christ, then you need to battle against Self-hatred, Guilt and the principality of Accusation. When thoughts of "God doesn't love me" overrun your mind, cast them down. "Let God be true and every man a liar."

> **God forbid: yea, let God be true, but every man a liar;** Romans 3:4

The Bible tells us we are to hold every thought captive, casting down every imagination, everything that exalts itself against the knowledge of God, and be ready to revenge all disobedience after our obedience is fulfilled.

> [5]Casting down imaginations, and every high thing that exalteth itself against the knowledge of God, and bringing into captivity every thought to the obedience of Christ;
> [6]And having in a readiness to revenge all disobedience, when your obedience is fulfilled.
> 2 Corinthians 10:5-6

There is a reason to holding every thought captive. It is to bring us to a progressive reality of overcoming.

STAGE THREE: DELIVERANCE

The next stage is deliverance. There is a certain group of people who will have knowledge and discernment and will go into absolute freedom instantly. But this does not always happen. When you are able to discern and know who you are in Christ and you have identified family curses, personal sins and evil thoughts, but are still in bondage, deliverance becomes necessary.

> [43]When the unclean spirit is gone out of a man, he walketh through dry places, seeking rest, and findeth none.
> [44]Then he saith, I will return into my house from whence I came out; and when he is come, he findeth *it* empty, swept, and garnished.
> [45]Then goeth he, and taketh with himself seven other spirits more wicked than himself, and they enter in and dwell there: and the last *state* of that man is worse than the first. Even so shall it be also unto this wicked generation.
> Matthew 12:43-45

You need the gifts operating at this point. The gifts are not there to replace knowledge and spiritual warfare. I have seen many people try to operate in gifts without these first two steps established in their life. Our minds must be subjected daily to God's way of thinking. Washing of water by the Word is necessary before, during and after deliverance from all indwelling sin because the enemy has programmed our minds.

> [26]That he might sanctify and cleanse it with the washing of water by the word,
> [27]That he might present it to himself a glorious church, not having spot, or wrinkle, or any such thing; but that it should be holy and without blemish. Ephesians 5:26-27

Sanctification

When something is being sanctified, there is smoke, friction and all kinds of stuff. The best thing that can happen is for it to surface so that it can be eliminated.

Timed Release in Sanctification

When God saved me, He saw everything that was unsanctified. He also knows all about timed release. I had one of those timed release things come to me recently. The enemy showed up one day. When he came, I was ready for him. I came into a place of discernment and there was a "No Vacancy" sign hanging. I was able to separate his thoughts from my thoughts and the Word. So I lined up with the knowledge of God and declared the enemy's thoughts to be inferior. I chose to have the mind of Christ.

You need to be taught how to walk as saints at this level because your greatest victory is just like Joshua the high priest experienced in Zechariah 3. You stand there and let the LORD clothe you in righteousness while the devil is at your right hand resisting you all the way.

The LORD Himself was there in Zechariah 3 and personally rebuked Satan. He then put a fair mitre on Joshua's head and clothed him. It was all invisible. Joshua the high priest stood there in victory.

> ¹And he shewed me Joshua the high priest standing before the angel of the LORD, and Satan standing at his right hand to resist him.
> ²And the LORD said unto Satan, The LORD rebuke thee, O Satan; even the LORD that hath chosen Jerusalem rebuke thee: *is* not this a brand plucked out of the fire?
> ³Now Joshua was clothed with filthy garments, and stood before the angel.
> ⁴And he answered and spake unto those that stood before him, saying, Take away the filthy garments from him. And unto him he said, Behold, I have caused thine iniquity to pass from thee, and I will clothe thee with change of raiment.
> ⁵And I said, Let them set a fair mitre upon his head. So they set a fair mitre upon his head, and clothed him with garments. And the angel of the Lord stood by.   Zechariah 3:1-5

Joshua was not removed from his office as high priest because he had dirty garments. The LORD did not listen to Satan and remove Joshua because he had sin. The LORD cleansed Joshua and released him to be the high priest.

When I started in ministry I had a battle with profanity. For a year and a half I had to struggle

Personality Mis-Profiles

through. I would be ministering healing in the name of Jesus and I would hear in my mind, #%*! Christ. When I was a sinner I had a few choice words, but nothing like I was hearing day after day.

After about 6 months of this I went before God and said, "You know it's not me. It's not *me*! It was a fiery dart" and it continued round the clock, 24 hours a day. Between every breath would be a vulgar word, no matter what I was doing.

I begged God to take it from me; I did spiritual warfare. I did everything I could think of and it would not leave. One day the Spirit of God rose up in my heart, and I told my enemy this: "Here's the deal. If I have to preach the gospel, heal the sick and cast out devils in the name of Jesus #%*! Christ, I'm going to do it. Every breath I have is going to be for Him, and every breath you have in between will be you. I'm going to serve the living God who called me."

It went on for 6 more months. Every bit of profanity and vulgarity you could think of would flood my consciousness, but I kept going. That was not who I was. A year and a half later I woke up one morning and it was gone. It has not come back for 20 years. That was timed release to intimidate me and steal the ordination of the living God from my life.

A few years ago someone was really nasty with me. He had some misguided information and said I was just a sinner. He discredited what I was doing in ministry and really hurt my feelings. One day I resolved myself to say to God, "If I'm deceived, not born again, not saved and a sinner, yet I'm out here preaching the gospel and doing all I see in the Word and I'm a fraud,

29

I'm still going to preach the gospel, heal the sick and cast out devils.

Can you go there? When the devil is tearing you apart, making you feel unclean, filthy and unrighteous can you preach the gospel in your filthiness of mind? When you can stand at this level in victory, you will experience a wonderful peace, the peace that passes all understanding.

God saved you for a reason. I do not care if Satan himself walks in the door with all of his whatever. You can stand there, look him straight in the eye and tell him you are going to be who God created you to be.

LIES VS. TRUTH

Jesus taught us who we are in the beatitudes. "Blessed are the merciful for they shall obtain mercy. Blessed are the pure in heart for they shall see God." You are salt. You are light. "Blessed are the peacemakers." I do not believe you have to go to heaven to be transformed because when you get to heaven you do not need to be transformed.

Do you think Paul needed to wait? Paul said, "From the foundation of the world, God ordained me to be an apostle to the Gentiles."

> For I speak to you Gentiles, inasmuch as I am the apostle of the Gentiles, I magnify mine office:
> Romans 11:13

> According as he hath chosen us in him before the foundation of the world, that we should be holy and without blame before him in love:
> Ephesians 1: 4

Personality Mis-Profiles

Look at King David. He got caught in his own lust. Yet we sing David's Psalms and quote his scriptures. He was a man after God's own heart.

Abraham had Fear of man and was a liar. He lied to the Pharaoh and to Abimelech the king of the Philistines. The father of our faith had spiritual problems, but God chose him to be the father of many nations anyway.

Not only did Abraham have a Lying spirit and Fear of man, his son Isaac inherited the same problems. Isaac and Rebecca went into the land of the Philistines where Abimelech was still king. Word for word, Isaac said what his father had said 40 years earlier, "This is not my wife; she's my sister." He yielded to Fear of man and an inherited Lying spirit.

It continued for four generations because 10 out of 12 sons of Jacob lied about what happened to Joseph. Exodus 20:5 says in the preamble to the 10 Commandments the sins of the fathers shall be passed on to the third and fourth generation. In spite of these four generations of sin, Abraham is called a friend of God.

In this teaching we stereotyped Abraham as a liar, but he is still called a friend of God. We really do not stereotype Abraham, Isaac and Jacob as liars. When you look back at David, do you consider him a murderer and an adulterer? Do you think he is a type of Christ—king, prophet and priest? We do because we consider him as the man the Word establishes him to be, after his conversion, according to selection, election and ordination. We see him the way God saw him from the foundation of the world.

God's greatest leaders were very imperfect. When God changed them, they were not that old man or that old woman, they became a new person. When you become that new creature in Christ, you are really not a new person; you are really just beginning to walk in what He intended for you from the foundation of the world.

The beginning of all healing is when you are able to separate yourself from the law of sin and apply your heart unto the law of God that is life. It is something you have to practice.

I lost 38 years of my life and I am not going to lose one more day to the devil on any level.

The Scripture says:

> ¹To the chief Musician, A Psalm of David. O LORD, thou hast searched me, and known *me*.
> ²Thou knowest my downsitting and mine uprising, thou understandest my thought afar off.
> ³Thou compassest my path and my lying down, and art acquainted *with* all my ways.
> ⁴For there *is* not a word in my tongue, *but*, lo, O LORD, thou knowest it altogether.
> ⁵Thou hast beset me behind and before, and laid thine hand upon me.
> ⁶*Such* knowledge *is* too wonderful for me; it is high, I cannot *attain* unto it.
> ⁷Whither shall I go from thy spirit? or whither shall I flee from thy presence?
> ⁸If I ascend up into heaven, thou *art* there: if I make my bed in hell, behold, thou *art there*.
> ⁹*If* I take the wings of the morning, *and* dwell in the uttermost parts of the sea;
> ¹⁰Even there shall thy hand lead me, and thy right hand shall hold me.
> ¹¹If I say, Surely the darkness shall cover me; even the night shall be light about me.

> ¹²Yea, the darkness hideth not from thee; but the night shineth as the day: the darkness and the light are both alike *to thee*.   Psalm 139:1-12

This scripture is exactly what we are talking about. It refers to standing in the midst of every thought and reality and having absolute peace even if it is in hell.

You should be able to stand in the midst of depression and not be depressed. You need to be able to stand in the midst of confusion and never be confused. You need to be able to stand in the midst of all disease and never, ever misunderstand health.

You need to be able to stand in the presence of all evil and

never misunderstand the goodness and life of God. That is what I find in Scripture as a sign of maturity.

"If I say, surely the darkness shall cover me, even the night shall be light about me. Yea, the darkness hideth from me, but the night shineth as the day." This is a powerful scripture against depression. Is darkness and light the same to you? Or are you buffeted by every thought and fiery dart that comes along?

Paul was buffeted, incredibly so, but he continued to serve God and subjected himself to the mind of Christ. He did not stereotype himself. He knew he was called to be an apostle of Jesus Christ in spite of his battle with sin.

> **For thou hast possessed my reins: thou hast covered me in my mother's womb.**   Psalm 139:13

That word "reins" means the innermost thoughts of your being. "You have covered me in my mother's womb." Jeremiah was covered, called, and sanctified before he was ever born (Jeremiah 1:5). In Psalm 139 David represents you and me. Even though you were born into original sin, as David tells us in Psalm 51, God was still there in the womb with you. You would not be saved today if He had not been there with you.

From the beginning, you were no accident or surprise. From the foundation of the world God ordained that you be saved and placed in your generation—and not just for part of it. I do not believe God calls people to check in and then check out. I believe God calls you to check in and stay checked-in!

There is no retirement age in God. Moses did not start his ministry until he was 80. He wasted 80 years of his life, 40 of it hiding in fear.

The psalmist says:

> [14]I will praise thee; for I am fearfully *and* wonderfully made: marvellous *are* thy works; and *that* my soul knoweth right well.
> [15]My substance was not hid from thee, when I was made in secret, *and* curiously wrought in the lowest parts of the earth.   Psalm 139:14-15

It is time to accept that God knew me from foundation of the world.

Do you believe that God loves you in your unrenewed state? Do you believe He loves you when the fiery darts are coming? Do you believe He loves you when stuff is there?

> **Thine eyes did see my substance, yet being unperfect; and in thy book all *my members* were**

written, *which* in continuance were fashioned, when *as yet there was* none of them. Psalm 139:16

Fabricated Personalities

As we struggle with our identity, many will dress up in defense mechanisms to avoid conflict or rejection. That is part of a fabricated personality. God has taught us we do not have to disguise ourselves; we have to be transparent. I do not find disguise used as a spiritual principle in Scripture—except for maybe King David, when he made believe he was insane in order to stay alive. That certainly was a defense mechanism. It saved him from a jam. However, turning insanity into a defense should not become a doctrine.

Sometimes when you talk to people, you may not be talking to the person. I think a good example is Marilyn Monroe. What you saw was not the real woman. Did you know that? The smile and glamour portrayed in those photographs was not who she was on the inside. The real woman was hurting; the real woman was devastated. That personality killed her.

What a sad tragedy. I am not overly impressed by what people say, how much they smile or what they bring initially. The Bible says you shall know them by their fruit. The fruit of their life will soon be evident. It does not take too long to figure out whether or not they are wearing a façade.

Wherefore by their fruits ye shall know them.
Matthew 7:20

Several years ago, a much tormented man came to us for ministry. He was an executive in a corporation, very successful and making good money, but he was struggling with insomnia and basically becoming "unglued." He tried magnetics in an attempt to establish peace in his body. However, the more he used it, the more tormented he became.

I had a conversation with him in ministry about his life history. He told me his father was a crass, coarse carnival worker who was always broke in spite of traveling and doing many road shows. The father took his young son with him sometimes when he traveled. Occasionally, he would take his son to very sexually immoral places. He considered this funny.

As this man grew up, he determined in his heart he would become the exact opposite of his father. It became a life exercise. He made a mental list of the 30 or 40 things he did not like about his dad. By the age of 35 he was the exact opposite of his dad, but he was much tormented.

One day in ministry I said to him, "I don't doubt you're born again and God loves you but for all practical purposes, as a human being, you don't exist. There's no peace in your life. There's no witness of the Spirit of God working in you. You're somewhere in there, but if being the opposite of your father was what God purposed for you from the foundation of the world, you would be in peace.

"Instead, I see you as a driven perfectionist trying to preserve some sort of identity. Any little problem that comes along is a threat to your very existence. You have not made any allowance for failure or weakness.

You have defense mechanisms in place to accommodate the things you have difficulty facing."

This sort of problem is very common in America today and is present in most churches. It is not easy to unravel. It involves taking a person almost from the womb and remaking them in their entire spirit and soul. It involves stripping everything that is not of God, including the desolation of the many generations they have inherited.

Then it includes asking God to remake them according to His image and His calling for them, bringing them back to a place of functionality in the living organism called the body of Christ. This is a tough battle. It can take some time, but it is a wonderful application of righteousness.

With regard to Multiple Personality Disorder (also called Dissociative Identity Disorder), the Christian church is into integration and fusion, which is no different than the approach used in clinical psychology and psychotherapy. The entire Christian church has bought Jung's lie from the spirit Philemon. Integration and fusion assume the fragmentation of the human personality is just different parts of the real person.

They take each of the personalities and bring them to the cross to get them to confess Jesus and become born again. They take every aspect of the break-off and attempt to integrate and fuse it back into one personality. This ultimately binds the person forever, as a human being, to all the fragmentation. They are taught to live with the tragedy and the fragmentation now as a whole person.

I have not found one person with Multiple Personality Disorder or DID who has ever been totally healed through integration and fusion. I find them tormented. They spend years and years in therapy trying to fuse all their personalities. It just does not work.

A woman came to us from San Francisco. She had been in therapy for more than 14 years attempting to fuse and integrate 14 or more personalities. After reviewing her history and interviewing these personalities, it took less than 30 seconds to remove the entities causing the multiples. She went back to San Francisco so her psychotherapist could verify her healing. I have a three-page letter from him confirming that she is well. We have had success with Multiple Personality Disorder/DID that is second to none in America.

If there is a split personality, I am against welding the split. I am for removing the part causing the split and leaving in place the true person God created. If there are fabricated personalities, I am interested in removing them and leaving in place the person God created from the foundation of the world: one single-minded person living in peace as the child God created them to be.

I believe true healing of the human psyche involves the removal of spirit entities at the spirit level. There is no other way I have been able to make it happen.

> [12]For the word of God *is* quick, and powerful, and sharper than any twoedged sword, piercing even to the dividing asunder of soul and spirit, and of the joints and marrow, and *is* a discerner of the thoughts and intents of the heart.
> [13]Neither is there any creature that is not manifest in his sight: but all things are naked and

opened unto the eyes of him with whom we have to do.   Hebrews 4:12-13

PERSONALITIES BY NATURE

Have you ever been around someone who had so much Rejection, you had to handle them with kid gloves all the time? You really had to choose your words because if you did not say it just right, they would flip out and go into Rejection. Have you ever seen someone that was dressed up in depression or even Fear?

I was asked to minister to a young girl at an airport during a layover. I spent about an hour and a half with this girl and her mother. When I sat down and started getting to know them, I looked into the daughter's eyes and saw many things. It did not take much. I did not need a word of knowledge; it was written all over her. She was wearing it and I knew where I had to go. She was dressed up in a personality of Fear.

It was not just that she had a spirit of Fear; she had a personality of Fear. Have you ever seen people who have phobias or panic attacks? These are personalities of Fear and phobias that have become ingrained in that person's life.

Have you ever been around someone who is dressed up in unloveliness and Rejection? They feel like second-rate citizens in the kingdom. They just know the other saints are barely putting up with them. They listen to the lies over and over again.

It is like a video camera playing the same video over and over, day after day, until they finally become one with it. Their soul and spirit become one according to the law of sin. Then someone comes along and stereotypes them. Now they have a handle to hang onto for the rest of their life identifying them with the fallen part of their nature. How tragic! They are bound to it and will declare, "This is just the way I am."

Now I do not know what the church is going to do with that. They tell you once you are born again you have no evil residing in you. Paul trashed that idea in Romans 7.

I believe what Paul had to say. I have begun my theology in Romans 7. It answered not only my questions, but it addressed a struggle in my own life. It gave me the first spiritual sanity I ever had. I finally understood that I was not the sin in me. What a revelation!

When I realized that stuff in me was of the devil, and I was still born again, that was incredibly liberating. Before understanding this I felt evil, yet I knew I had a heart towards God. I am not evil. God knew that when He saved me. He knew I had a heart for Him.

You are not evil, either. God knows you have a heart for Him. He knows it; so do not listen to lies. I may do some squirrelly things that may be evil, but I am going to take responsibility for them. Did David take responsibility for his sin? Yes. Did Saul take responsibility for his sin? No.

What separates you from the rest of the boys and girls in the kingdom of God is not that you have sin, but what you do with it when you discern it. God wants us cleaned up: scrub-a-dub-dub, a bunch of saints in a tub.

> **As the bird by wandering, as the swallow by flying, so the curse causeless shall not come.**
> Proverbs 26:2

A personality of Self-rejection, Self-hatred and Guilt may have transferred into you in your youth. It may have come from sexual molestation or from a father and mother who did not say they loved you. It may have come from a husband or wife. It may have come from some saint in the church who said you had spiritual halitosis. The transference of an unclean spirit into your nature could have come from anywhere, and then you became one with it.

When you find disease in the spiritual, psychological or biological realm, there is an open door that needs identifying. Satan has a legal right to your life in spite of what Jesus did at the cross. That is your turf. That is your area of renewal, restoration and sanctification. That is the area you are working out daily with fear and trembling.

MIND/BODY CONNECTION

The enemy's lies of unloveliness, guilt and fear start working through you as thoughts, feelings, impressions and pictures. The more you listen to them, the louder they become. Your mind becomes programmed. These thoughts control you not just from the spiritual dimension, but now also from the psychological dimension.

It can take days, weeks, months or even years until the mind-body connection senses trouble back upstream via the hypothalamus gland. The hypothalamus is the brain of the endocrine system. It integrates the autonomic nervous system along with the secretion of hormones and various neurotransmitters.

You are very chemical in your creation. The inside of your body is nothing more than a bunch of little chemical plants manufacturing various chemicals, hormones and neurotransmitters God designed to maintain basic homeostasis. Your enemy knows he can interrupt and cause an aberration of the secretion of hormones, chemicals and neurotransmitters by controlling your thoughts.

For every thought you have, conscious or unconscious, there is a corresponding chemical released somewhere in the human body to activate the consequence of the fruit of that thought. As you are in conflict with yourself, believing all the lies, struggling with thoughts, voices and pictures, the pineal gland, which is the main gland for the regulation of the secretion of serotonin, will either under- or oversecrete serotonin.

Serotonin

Serotonin is also a facilitator of your thoughts. When it is oversecreted, in conjunction with norepinephrine and dopamine, it creates an aberration in thought that produces paranoid schizophrenia. When serotonin is undersecreted, it produces feelings such as lack of self-esteem and guilt with respect to love and nurturing. In anxiety, for example, there is not enough serotonin secreted. There is a breakdown so the person feels really agitated and does not feel good about himself. He is nervous and jerky about everything.

The mechanisms are just incredible. We become one with the Unloving spirit. We become one with the Guilt. We become one with the lack of self-esteem. The body responds as we agree with these unclean spirits. The hypothalamus gland senses trouble. The pineal gland responds by stopping the secretion of serotonin.

Now, not only do you have the thought telling you that you are a failure or you are no good, you have the physiological feeling to reinforce those lies. You have been had on all three dimensions: spiritually, psychologically and biologically.

I think we have been able to document almost 500 different personality aberrations in mankind that are spiritual. This would include Fear, Bitterness, Self-rejection, Self-hatred, just to name a few. They all have a specific fruit which long-term produces most of our diseases. Not all disease has a spiritual root directly, but many do.

One of the most powerful things about our ministry is we know how and where the devil is working to destroy man, and we know the consequences. It is no longer a mystery. You do not need a word of knowledge. It is just that obvious. It is the same in most diseases. The devil is the same yesterday, today and tomorrow. If you have seen one, you have seen them all.

If I could tell you that you had depression because of an unloving, unclean spirit of Rejection, would that be significant to you? If I could tell you that you had a certain mental torment because of Fear and Anxiety, would that be significant to you? If I could give you the etiology of your problem spiritually, would that be significant to you?

Well, it would be the only thing that makes any sense because otherwise you are lost in the mess of your own thoughts, emotions and feelings with no way out. You are lost in the ignorance of the moment, and your enemy is controlling your very physiology and soul.

You are in a prison house with no way out until the truth of God's Word gives you insight and discernment. That is why the Word of God is a discerner of the thoughts and intents of the heart. This is the level of knowledge and discernment the church needs today — not only to heal disease, but to prevent it. Being able to discern both good and evil is a sign of maturity.

> **But strong meat belongeth to them that are of full age,** *even* **those who by reason of use have their senses exercised to discern both good and evil.** Hebrews 5:14

MOTIVE OF THE HEART

God looks at the motive of the heart. God's perfect will is not to heal you. His perfect will is that you do not get sick. I think the Christian church can teach disease prevention very easily by teaching sanctification, though not from a legalistic standpoint. You can do works of righteousness, but your heart can still be far from God.

The curse will still come. Did you know that? It is not your action that produces or moves the hand of God; it is your heart toward the sin that moves the hand of God. So if you try to be righteous to keep from getting disease, you have no protection whatsoever. If you want to be righteous because you love God and you know He loves you, then there is protection.

Dead Works vs. Fruit of the Spirit

Dead works get in the way of the fruit of the Spirit. Galatians says,

> ²²But the fruit of the Spirit is love, joy, peace, longsuffering, gentleness, goodness, faith,
> ²³Meekness, temperance: against such there is no law. Galatians 5:22-23

When I first came to the Lord, I looked up the entire meaning of each of the fruits of the Spirit and stuck them on my refrigerator. Every day I would stare at all those meanings. I would say, "God, that's beautiful. Is that Who You are? Is that why You saved me so I could be changed and my nature could be like this?" (For an in-depth study on Galatians 5:19-21, see *From the Inside/Out* in the Be in Health™ bookstore.)

It is, but we have a problem. Dead works get in the way. Bitterness steals your joy. Unforgiveness robs your peace. Fear will not let you receive love or give love.

First John says,

> There is no fear in love; but perfect love casteth out fear: because fear hath torment. He that feareth is not made perfect in love. 1 John 4:18

If you do not feel loved, Fear comes. "He that feareth is not made perfect in love." What does that mean? If you have this kind of breakdown in love, you are not able to give and receive love without Fear. Do you ever struggle with that? Oh you can give love, but how about receiving it? If I just took you in my arms and held you, would you squirm?

I sometimes go up to people and hold them like I would a child. Even adult men! This is not an unclean action. John laid his head on Jesus' breast, and they were not unclean in their relationship. I love challenging men at this level. I will grab hold of a man and tell him I want to count to 100. I will count very slowly: "One, two, three."

He starts squirming and getting fidgety. "Four…" and he gets even more fidgety because he has Rejection and not love as part of his nature.

I get to 5 and he thinks, Oh my goodness he's going for it. "Six." Now I know I have him because he is really starting to move. "Six and a quarter… Six and a half."

He thinks, Oh, no! Pastor has broken it down into fractions. Get this man away from me!

Then I release him because he cannot handle it.

My father was a minister, but I was very rejected and abused emotionally, physically and verbally. I had an Unloving spirit. I was so full of Fear if someone came to the door, I would shake like a leaf, just like I had palsy. I could not look you in the eye. I would look at your nose or your feet or somewhere on the tree next door. Today people wish I would quit looking them in the eye!

When I was saved, I was part of a large charismatic church. God placed me there to get my feet wet. They were a radical bunch. There was an elder in that church who would hug me every Sunday. He had to have heard God because he would hold of me and not let go. He would sque-e-eze, and I would squi-r-r-rm. This person was no flake. He was a very fine, serious man of God. I respected him immensely.

It seemed every time I would come into the service, he was there in the doorway. There would be people coming and going and he would get me. He would hold on and just sque-e-eze me and I would think, "Oh no!" When I came in, I'd look for him so I could avoid him. I could not stand it. I was dressed up in Rejection.

I had a personality of Rejection and thought it was me. I thought it was just the way I was, tormented. I would go in a different door. He would see me and go there. "Oh, no!" This went on for about nine months. I almost quit going to church because I couldn't handle it.

Then one day when I came in and he grabbed me, all of a sudden God did a work in my heart. The Unloving spirit's power was broken. As he held me, I went limp and melted right into his arms. I found myself hugging him. I held him until *he* was screaming to get away! I have been hugging people ever since.

I realized in my heart this man really cared for me. Perfect love casts out Fear.

Doctrines of Christ

Hebrews says,

> Therefore leaving the principles of the doctrine of Christ, let us go on unto perfection;

> not laying again the foundation of repentance from dead works, and of faith toward God,
>
> Hebrews 6:1

We are supposed to leave the principles of the doctrines of Christ and go on to perfection. This means something needs to have been established.

REPENTANCE FROM DEAD WORKS

This scripture clearly tells that the first principle that needs to be mastered is Repentance. This is number one and there is no need to go further. But what did we do? We read further in the verse and jumped on down to faith towards God. So we created the faith movement. And we created the Word movement. There is nothing wrong with the faith or Word movement, but some have skipped the first part which is repentance from dead works.

You can have all the faith you want toward God. You can know all the Word you want, but if you do not have a repentant heart and crucify the flesh, it produces nothing but self-righteousness and religion. We are saying all the right things, but our hearts are still evil toward God.

Why doesn't faith toward God come before Repentance from dead works? The Word tells us our sins have separated us from God. Our sins will separate us from the *faith* of God.

If you are going to deal with this, do not worry so much about having faith in God. First, understand sanctification, and then your ability to have faith in God

PERSONALITY MIS-PROFILES

will increase proportionately. I think there is an importance to the order of the words.

Repent and believe the gospel. Mark 1:15

Dead works are the fruit of unrighteousness. What are dead works? Fear is a dead work. Does Fear produce anything productive as far as God is concerned? No. What else is a dead work? Unbelief, Self-hatred, Guilt, Rage and Anger, and others.

Mark says,

> **15There is nothing from without a man, that entering into him can defile him: but the things which come out of him, those are they that defile the man...**
> **20And he said, That which cometh out of the man, that defileth the man.**
> **21For from within, out of the heart of men, proceed evil thoughts, adulteries, fornications, murders,**
> **22Thefts, covetousness, wickedness, deceit, lasciviousness, an evil eye, blasphemy, pride, foolishness:**
> **23All these evil things come from within, and defile the man.** Mark 7:15, 20-23

From the heart of men proceed evil thoughts. Have saints ever had evil thoughts?

James outlines the 7 steps to sin.

> **14But every man is tempted, when he is drawn away of his own lust, and enticed.**
> **15Then when lust hath conceived, it bringeth forth sin: and sin, when it is finished, bringeth forth death.** James 1:14-15

A thought or temptation is not sin. So someone can be tempted in lust and never sin in it. The Word also says if a man looks on a woman and lusts after her in his heart, he has committed adultery already.

There is a conclusion of the heart that comes to fruition, becoming part of a person's nature before the act is ever done. Evil thoughts can become part of our nature spiritually and psychologically. Or, you can have an evil thought, and it is just temptation.

To make an evil thought part of your way of thinking long-term means you would at some point have to *accept* it. When an evil thought becomes part of your thinking permanently, it lays a foundation for performing that thought. It is now a conclusion: a spiritual foundation that is now part of you. This thought has become part of your personality. It is no longer a temptation; it has become an accepted part of your nature.

Now dead works are these: evil thoughts, adulteries, fornications, murders, thefts, covetousness, wickedness, deceit, lasciviousness, an evil eye, blasphemy, pride, foolishness. All these things come from within and defile you. That evil has become part of your nature. When it comes up, you go down. It fulfills itself and then you are the one that has to pay the penalty for it.

It is like what happens to someone who commits murder and goes to prison. There was a spirit of Murder coming out of Bitterness that manifested and acted through the man or woman. He or she committed murder, was arrested and put in jail for the rest of their life. Meanwhile, the evil spirit of Murder was laughing all the way from hell. The person pays the penalty for the act because that part of their nature, a spirit of Murder, had become one with them.

Dead Works

In Romans it says God gives people up to vile affections:

> For this cause God gave them up unto vile affections: Romans 1:26

The following are some dead works and there are many more. You may have 238 in you today. I used to have 369. I am down to 127.

> [29]Being filled with all unrighteousness, fornication, wickedness, covetousness, maliciousness; full of envy, murder, debate, deceit, malignity; whisperers,
> [30]Backbiters, haters of God, despiteful, proud, boasters, inventors of evil things, disobedient to parents,
> [31]Without understanding, covenant breakers, without natural affection, implacable, unmerciful:
> [32]Who knowing the judgment of God, that they which commit such things are worthy of death, not only do the same, but have pleasure in them that do them. Romans 1:29-32

There are not degrees of sin. Let's get that straight. There are not white sins and dark sins.

> For all have sinned, and come short of the glory of God; Romans 3:23

That means all of us have fallen short of His nature and perfection. Whoever is guilty in one point of law is guilty of all. That is why we need a Savior.

> Ye that love the Lord, hate evil: he preserveth the souls of his saints; he delivereth them out of the hand of the wicked. Psalm 97:10

In Galatians dead works are identified as:

> ¹⁹Now the works of the flesh are manifest, which are *these*; Adultery, fornication, uncleanness, lasciviousness,
> ²⁰Idolatry, witchcraft, hatred, variance, emulations, wrath, strife, seditions, heresies,
> ²¹Envyings, murders, drunkenness, revellings, and such like: Galatians 5:19-21

Strife is thrown right in with murder, hatred, fornication, adultery and drunkenness. Do you think strife is in the Christian church today? How about in our homes?

What are seditions? Undermining of authority. Church splits. People that rise up with a spirit like the one behind Korah. I have not found one church split ever to be blessed by God.

What are heresies? Heresy is anything which changes the Word of God into a lie. Heresy is the doctrine of devils. Heresy is anything that does not match what God has revealed in His Word in simple terms so even a child can understand.

If you do not repent from dead works they will become part of your personality. What you lend yourself to becomes your master. You are called to be a slave of Jesus Christ unto righteousness.

> ...of the which I tell you before, as I have also told *you* in time past, that they which do such things shall not inherit the kingdom of God. Galatians 5:21

If you habitually do these things as a way of life with a hardened heart, you shall not inherit the kingdom of God.

> [19]Surely thou wilt slay the wicked, O God: depart from me therefore, ye bloody men.
> [20]For they speak a gainst thee wickedly, *and* thine enemies take *thy name* in vain.
> [21]Do not I hate them, O LORD, that hate thee? and am not I grieved with those that rise up against thee?
> [22]I hate them with perfect hatred: I count them mine enemies.
> [23]Search me, O God, and know my heart: try me, and know my thoughts:
> [24]And see *if there be any* wicked way in me, and lead me in the way everlasting.
> Psalm139:19-24

You cannot put new wine in old wine skins because the ball of fermentation called the "mother" has left a residue of fermentation in the wine skin. This fermentation represents the decaying process of death. If you put the new wine into the old skin, the new wine will be affected. The new wine does not change the old skin; the old skin affects the new wine. It is amazing how death affects life on that basis.

If you allow the aspects of what the old wine skin represents to stay within you, it will infect and cause a defect in your human spirit. That is why Paul told us to crucify our flesh. That is what circumcision of the heart is all about. You are putting to death something that is putting you to death. Being born again is more than just going to heaven. It is a complete reversal of everything death represents while you are still alive—every bit of it because it is a plague.

Fear is contagious. Bitterness is contagious. Hatred is contagious. Strife is contagious. Sedition is contagious. Look at Korah and the 250 elders of Israel. Look at one-third of all angels that listened to Lucifer and his rebellion. Do you think rebellion is contagious?

One-third of all angels rebelled with Lucifer against the God that created them. Do you think sin is contagious? Absolutely! The body of Christ needs to be purified. We need to check the condition of the wine skin — not collectively, but individually.

We want our churches to be so spiritual, yet the church is nothing. The people make it spiritual. You cannot have a spiritual church unless you have spiritual people in it.

> **Having therefore these promises, dearly beloved, let us cleanse ourselves from all filthiness of the flesh and spirit, perfecting holiness in the fear of God.** 2 Corinthians 7:1

Some say, "Well if God wants me different, He's just going to have to come down and change me here." The fact is that we are not just robots of righteousness.

Deuteronomy says to choose this day what you shall have: blessings or curses, life or death.

> **I call heaven and earth to record this day against you, *that* I have set before you life and death, blessing and cursing: therefore choose life, that both thou and thy seed may live:** Deuteronomy 30:19

There is a movement of your sovereignty to which we have to pay attention. I want you to be well. I am not trying to teach you theology; I am trying to teach you foundations of truth so you can get the curse off your poor head and spirit and God can bless you.

Ezekiel says,

> Yet ye say, The way of the Lord is not equal...
> Ezekiel 18:25

This statement in Ezekiel is made by Adonay, the Father.

> ²⁵Yet ye say, The way of the Lord is not equal. Hear now, O house of Israel; Is not my way equal? are not your ways unequal?
> ²⁶When a righteous *man* turneth away from his righteousness, and committeth iniquity, and dieth in them; for his iniquity that he hath done shall he die.
> ²⁷Again, when the wicked *man* turneth away from his wickedness that he hath committed, and doeth that which is lawful and right, he shall save his soul alive.
> Ezekiel 18:25-27

Israel is taking God on for size about His righteousness and His position with them concerning their sin. They are accusing Adonai of not being fair because God was forgiving unrighteous repenters, but would not forgive His own people Israel who would not repent.

Israel did not like it. They wanted God to condone their sin. They accused God because the curse came on them, God's covenant people. The curse did not just come on New Testament people. The evidence is overwhelming. Or are we just in denial?

Both the righteous and the unrighteous commit sin. The righteous shall die when they turn away from following God. The wages of sin is still death. When you are sanctified there is nothing to interfere with blessing. If we are obedient to God and His Word then no curses will come upon us.

> But it shall come to pass, if thou wilt not hearken unto the voice of the LORD thy God, to observe to do all his commandments and his statutes which I command thee this day; that all these curses shall come upon thee, and overtake thee: Deuteronomy 28:15

So when the Bible says to love yourself as you love your neighbor, what are you going to do? Love yourself. When the Bible says you have not been given a spirit of Fear, what are you going to do with Fear? Cast it down as a lying imagination!

When you are following the Spirit of God and Condemnation and Guilt come along, what are you going to do? Rebuke them. Trash them. When you are following the lust of the flesh, what are you going to do? Repent because He is faithful and just to forgive you your sins and cleanse you from all unrighteousness.

> If we confess *our* sins, he is faithful and just to forgive us *our* sins, and to cleanse us from all unrighteousness. 1 John 1:9

Apply the Word Daily

Do you ever apply the Scriptures to life at this level? Well, you need to. You need to see Scripture as it really is in pragmatic, day-to-day, down-to-earth application. Hold every thought captive. Cast down every imagination that would exalt itself against the knowledge of God.

You do not have to become split in your personality, where one part of you is of God and one part of you is not renewed. You can become one in the knowledge of who you are in God.

I was at a meeting in Atlanta with about 140 pastors from all over America and Canada. This group of pastors had been involved with the renewal and prophetic movement and had invited a sociologist to make a presentation. She had been studying the movement of the Holy Spirit for many years. She gave the renewal a "D" internationally and said it had become introspective and inverted. Rather than impacting the world around it, this movement only impacted those who were sucked into its tunnel. She said a true move of God should impact the world.

I reminded these pastors of what she had said when I taught that evening. They were not too happy with the grade they received. I took them to Romans and quoted this scripture:

> **For the kingdom of God is not meat and drink; but righteousness, and peace, and joy in the Holy Ghost.** Romans 14:17

I told those 140 pastors, "You received a 'D' because you went to joy in the Holy Ghost, but you forgot the rest of the Godhead. The true move of God producing joy in the Holy Ghost is through the first two members of the Godhead. You cannot put new wine into old wineskins."

Righteousness Represents the Father

Righteousness represents the Father. Our righteousness is *of* the Father. God is the Father of all spirits.

> **And they fell upon their faces, and said, O God, the God of the spirits of all flesh, ...**
> Numbers 16:22

I taught to a diminishing audience with only fifteen out of 140 left listening. The point I tried to make was that God is not interested in bringing to the world a score of "D." He is interested in bringing a score of 100 or an "A."

I was teaching them although joy in the Holy Ghost is something we need and I was not putting it down, you cannot stay in joy in the Holy Ghost at the expense of not teaching righteousness and peace. You cannot just center on the Holy Ghost because the Father is going to get ticked off. Besides, the Holy Spirit does not even speak of Himself. He honors the Father and Word. He is in place to execute the will of the Father and the Word of God.

Peace Comes from Jesus the WORD

Where does peace come from? Jesus. Jesus said, "Peace give I unto you, but not as the world gives, give I unto you." Perfect peace belongs to those whose minds are stayed or fixed on the Lord.

> **Peace I leave with you, my peace I give unto you: not as the world giveth, give I unto you. Let not your heart be troubled, neither let it be afraid.**
> John 14:27

> Thou wilt keep *him* in perfect peace, *whose* mind *is* stayed *on thee*: because he trusteth in thee. Isaiah 26:3

What does the Word of God do for you? I tell you what it does for me. It brings peace to my heart. It is like a flashlight in the middle of my darkness.

If we center just on the Holy Spirit, we will center on experience to the exclusion of the Father and the Word. That is ungodly and out of order. We need to cultivate the fullness of the Godhead in our lives. Our nature is not just one of experience; our nature is balanced with the fullness of the Godhead.

Fellowship with the Godhead

We need to be in fellowship with all three members of the eternal Godhead, not just one or two of them. The Spirit of God will only honor the known will of the Father and the Word of God. The Spirit of God does not raise a standard against the enemy without the Word. Jesus defeated the devil with the Word of God. Do not ever forget it! He said, "For it is written…"

The Holy Spirit does not act upon the will or Word of God apart from your obedience. You may think: if I will confess this scripture three times a day, then God will do this. If I will do this, then God will do that. It is not a mantra. It is not the confession of the scripture that moves the hand of God; it is your *obedience* to that scripture.

The Blessings of Obedience

God blesses obedience, not rebellion. He is under no obligation to honor His Word in my life if I do not submit my heart to it. God has no obligation to do anything for me just because I know the Word. He is not going to bless me in my rebellion. He is only going to bless me in my obedience.

If it is legalism to keep God's commandments, then Jesus was the greatest legalist of all because He said, "If you love me, you will keep my commandments." Legalism is forcing someone to keep God's commandments. Jesus never did that to anyone. He may say to you: Even though you love me like Peter did and you blow it, when you have recovered yourself, strengthen the brethren.

I have observed our enemy. Just as God leads us progressively in His calling, the devil can also lead us progressively in our destruction. God leads us progressively in helping us work out our own salvation daily. He brings us into what He called us to be from the foundation of the world. The devil has his plan. It drives us down pathways of bondage and destruction.

The Enemy and Timed Release

The enemy does what I call timed release. Timed release is like the pill I used to take that quietly worked in my body until it exploded and did its thing in a really big way. Your enemy has something called timed release for you. The height of your glory is the height of your temptation; the greater the glory, the greater the fiery darts. If you are not aware of this, you'll fall right through the cracks.

BLACK AND WHITE

You need to be careful not to think in black and white. It is a trap. Have you ever been caught in black and white thinking? Black represents all that Satan's evil could ever be, and white represents all the good you could be in God. God in His perfection is to the far right and Satan in his total imperfection is to the far left. Guess who is caught in the middle? You are.

But are you all black? Are you all white? What are you? You are gray. Your enemy wants to remind you of who God is and who you are supposed to be in Him. He will show you the white and then he will show you the black in your life. He will make you feel so black you cannot appoint yourself unto righteousness. God accepts you by faith in your gray areas.

A Lighter Gray

Does that mean you are going to stay dark gray? No, because you have a heart for God. Sometimes, as we are working out our own salvation daily with fear and trembling, it is like climbing a greased pole. I would like to give you something to hang onto so the greased pole is easier to climb. Three steps forward and two steps backward is still forward progress.

Three steps forward
and two steps backward
is still forward progress

The Holy Spirit can give you things to hang onto that He anoints and confirms from Scripture. You do not need to be intimidated about this journey of renewal. He will encourage and empower you as you claw your way higher and higher every day.

In fact, you can rejoice in your tribulations and even in the un-renewed parts of your life. It is possible to rejoice in the darkness of your gray because you know where you are going. Just because you are not there does not mean you are not going there. Just show up and get in the right lane. God will move you in the direction you need to go.

I would rather be weary from defeating the devil than wasted and worn out from losing to him. I still have to work out my own salvation daily. If you were to look at my rap sheet from my "BC" days, you would need to have a long piece of paper. I know what I have been saved from.

Our Relationship with Others

Galatians says,

> [1]Brethren, if a man be overtaken in a fault, ye which are spiritual, restore such an one in the spirit of meekness; considering thyself, lest thou also be tempted.
> [2]Bear ye one another's burdens, and so fulfil the law of Christ.   Galatians 6:1-2

Jesus said, "I only say the things that I heard my Father say." Jesus the Word was the total mind of God the Father. When I read the beatitudes, I see Jesus did not teach about prophecy and gifts; He taught about how to love God, love your neighbor and love yourself. He taught you relationship at the horizontal and vertical levels.

The entire beatitudes have to do with down-to-earth living, without torment, division or error. This is restoring saints back to what God created them to be.

THE ROLE OF PASTOR

Allopathic medicine tries to sanctify you in the physio, or body. Psychology tries to sanctify you in the psyche, or soul. But who is sanctifying the human spirit these days? It is the role of the pastor and the body of Christ. They are the only ones qualified.

A breakdown in the spirit produces a breakdown in body and soul. But isn't it tragic that most pastors in America handle biological and psychological problems by subbing out their sheep to those trained in the worldly investigation of the soul and physiology or body? They do not consider the spiritual foundation of our problems. You cannot fix the spirit by fixing the physio (body) and you cannot fix the psyche (soul) without dealing with the spirit. You will just be moving fruit around.

> **And the very God of peace sanctify you wholly; and *I pray God* your whole spirit and soul and body be preserved blameless unto the coming of our Lord Jesus Christ.**
> 1 Thessalonians 5:23

> He that committeth sin is of the devil; for the devil sinneth from the beginning. For this purpose the Son of God was manifested, that he might destroy the works of the devil.   1 John 3:8
>
> How God anointed Jesus of Nazareth with the Holy Ghost and with power: who went about doing good, and healing all that were oppressed of the devil; for God was with him.   Acts 10:38
>
> 24 And the servant of the Lord must not strive; but be gentle unto *all* men, apt to teach, patient,
> 25 In meekness instructing those that oppose themselves; if God peradventure will give them repentance to the acknowledging of the truth;
> 26 And *that* they may recover themselves out of the snare of the devil, who are taken captive by him at his will.   2 Timothy 2:24-26

The Church and Healing of the Body

I talked with the wife of a church leader. She had been struggling for awhile with some things in her life and had not become free. Pastors and their wives go through stuff, too. She said to me, "Pastor, my husband is well known and I am alone in loneliness."

The body of Christ does not understand what the body of Christ is all about! The biggest need of the body is to figure out it was designed to heal and to take care of the body. Here is the problem. It is called Fear of man, Fear of rejection, Fear of failure, and Fear of abandonment. There is one common word: *Fear*.

Fear of Man

> 28 And fear not them which kill the body, but are not able to kill the soul: but rather fear him

which is able to destroy both soul and body in hell.

²⁹Are not two sparrows sold for a farthing? and one of them shall not fall on the ground without your Father.

³⁰But the very hairs of your head are all numbered.

³¹Fear ye not therefore, ye are of more value than many sparrows.

³²Whosoever therefore shall confess me before men, him will I confess also before my Father which is in heaven. Matthew 10:28-32

Fear of Rejection

²⁹And Jesus answered and said, Verily I say unto you, There is no man that hath left house, or brethren, or sisters, or father, or mother, or wife, or children, or lands, for my sake, and the gospel's,

³⁰But he shall receive an hundredfold now in this time, houses, and brethren, and sisters, and mothers, and children, and lands, with persecutions; and in the world to come eternal life. Mark 10:29-30

What shall we then say to these things? If God be for us, who *can be* against us? Romans 8:31

Fear of Failure

For a just *man* falleth seven times, and riseth up again: but the wicked shall fall into mischief.
Proverbs 24:16

Fear of Abandonment

Let *your* conversation *be* without covetousness; *and be* content with such things as

> ye have: for he hath said, I will never leave thee, nor forsake thee. Hebrews 13:5

> A man *that hath* friends must shew himself friendly: and there is a friend *that* sticketh closer than a brother. Proverbs 18:24

Our position in ministry is clear. No matter what sin issue you are dealing with, whether be it bestiality, murder, abortion, slander, homosexuality, adultery, fornication or whatever sin you can find in Romans 1, Galatians 5, Mark 7 or anywhere else in the Word, if you will come and humble yourself before the mighty hand of God in those areas, we will not attach you to that memory of the past. The Word of God says, "If we confess our sins, He is faithful and just to forgive us our sins and to cleanse us from all unrighteousness."

> If we confess our sins, he is faithful and just to forgive us our sins, and to cleanse us from all unrighteousness. 1 John 1:9

God the Father's thinking is the standard I must apply here. I will not attach to you any failures in your past nor will I stereotype you according to your past. I will rejoice because you are now matching what God created you to be from the foundation of the world. I will rejoice with you forever!

The book of Psalms says,

> As far as the east is from the west, *so* far hath he removed our transgressions from us. Psalm 103:12

If you have to walk with this un-renewed part of your life, why can't I walk with you? Should I withdraw from you until you are cleaned up? I cannot serve you if I do not join myself to you. This moves you into the kingdom of God while various aspects of you are still un-renewed. It is bringing you back into fellowship with God and others. If you are not honest with me, there is no fellowship.

Jesus said to Peter, "Satan desires to sift you like wheat." Why did Satan desire to sift him like wheat? Peter had some un-renewed, unsanctified parts of his nature that gave Satan access to his life. He had spiritual defects to the degree that at one point Jesus turned to him and said, "Satan, get thee behind me." Peter listened to lies and savored the things of men rather than of God. Jesus did not stereotype Peter. He told Peter, "When you have recovered yourself, strengthen the brethren."

Did Peter lose his salvation because he denied Christ? No, Jesus ordained him a second time after His resurrection. When Jesus found Peter fishing, He asked him three times, "Do you love me?"

Peter responded, "Oh, Lord you know I love you; why are you asking me these difficult questions?"

Jesus affirmed Peter and said, "Feed my sheep."

When we walk transparently before God, just the way we are with the good and the evil at whatever level it is, the blood of Jesus is available to cleanse us from all unrighteousness. Dare we trust each other at this level?

> **But if we walk in the light, as he is in the light, we have fellowship one with another, and the blood of Jesus Christ his Son cleanseth us from all sin.** 1 John 1:7

I had an exchange with a lady who was on the governing board in my church. She said she thought there was a breach between us. She did not feel comfortable. She asked me if I thought there was anything between us. I looked straight at her and said, "Yes there is something between us. You're right; you sensed it."

She asked what it was.

I said, "I wonder what you would be like if I ever did anything wrong. That's probably my concern. I don't have confidence that you'll cover me." She did not say anything. Within 6 months she was gone from my church and our board.

What are we going to do with each other when we find "rust spots?" Will I hear about it tomorrow morning on the news? The Word says to confess your faults one to another so you may be healed. It does not say to confess to the priest, prophet or pastor. It does not say you are going to be healed when you confess, but it sets the foundation for healing to come.

If we can meet each other at this level Satan has no power over us. There is no darkness. But if we feel the need to be perfect with each other, we are right back in a caste system with all those fear issues.

Paul identified in Romans 7 his struggle with sin. In today's world, many would label him as having a split personality. If we went to psychiatric terms, he would be labeled a borderline personality. He also was a murderer in the name of God, and the Scriptures indicate the Christian Jews in Jerusalem never fully trusted or accepted him after conversion. They judged him by his "BC" days. They could not understand conversion.

When I was on Christian radio many years ago, I used to have fun with my audience. I wanted to challenge them in their stereotyped thinking. I asked them if they thought Isaiah was born again. I would ask, "Do you think he was anointed of God?"

The question was framed around the details in Isaiah 20. God's people were guilty of looking to other nations for support against their enemies. They had to go to the strong arm of man instead of God. When you were defeated in war and taken alive, the custom was to take a knife and cut off the back part of your clothing, leaving your "behinder" parts exposed. It was an extremely shaming experience.

God told Isaiah because His people had put their trust in the strong arm of man, they would go back into captivity. He further told Isaiah, "I want you to walk naked up and down the land of Israel for three years as a sign of my contempt for my people putting their trust in a nation."

I asked my radio audience if Isaiah would be allowed in many churches. In most churches today people would scream, "What? Prophet Isaiah's coming to town? Not in my church!" Isaiah walked around naked for 3 years.

David's wife Michal had a similar reaction to David when he danced before the ark. Did she stereotype David? "How dare you jump! You're the king, act like it."

As we get involved with different sects of Christianity, it is educational and enlightening. We observe various denominations and their different ways of thinking spiritually. It helps us to have a broader scope of how God thinks. We can learn from everyone.

I need everyone; I do not have all the answers. I told one of my pastors the other day, "I really need you." There are things in him I do not have, and there are things in others I need. There may be something in me that *you* need. Not one person, not one denomination, not one church has the whole answer, but if we could ever pull this thing together, we would be dynamite in the world.

Conclusion

If you teach any aspect of the human brain as being the final and only basis of rationale and action, you have erred. The Bible says, "As a man thinketh in his heart, so is he." Not as he thinks in his brain! I can be bird-brained (forget about being left brained or right brained) and the thoughts of the living God within my spirit can still rule me.

Your thoughts do not determine who you are exclusively. This is another form of astrology. I can be ruled by the Spirit of God in spite of my rebellion, sin, thoughts and any un-renewed part of me. The Holy Spirit can lead me as a son of God by faith in the midst of it. I reserve the right to be spiritual, not just soulish or intellectual.

If you are not careful, you will make God and yourself into intellectual, soulish beings. This type of thinking is a form of psychology because it negates the human spirit. God is the God of all flesh, but He is also the Father of all spirits. If you go exclusively into the soulish realm, you will become trapped in your very own thoughts.

But God's thoughts are higher than my thoughts; His ways are higher than my ways. I want to release myself back to my spirit man where God the Holy Spirit lives and release myself to God according to the Word in spite of my poor brain.

If we are not careful, we will whitewash our spirit man. We do not want to create an intellectual religion because that is what happened to the Pharisees. Christianity is a religion of the spirit, not of the soul. I know your mind needs to be renewed by the washing of the water of the Word. That is very important, but our God is a spirit. Those who worship Him must worship Him in Spirit and in Truth.

You must come to that place where your spirit man is alive unto God. You must hope to God your mind catches up one day! So if you do not mind, I reserve the right to be a triune being.

When you die your body goes to the dust, but your spirit, according to Ecclesiastes, goes back to God. The spirit of the animal goes back to the dust, but the spirit of man goes back to God. Can our soul be saved if it goes back to dust?

In long-term memory, millions of pictures are taken similar to an electrochemical flash. That electrochemical reality in long-term memory integrates with something called protein synthesis, which is a factor of DNA and RNA. All of this becomes a physiological reality in your brain cells. Your memory is now preserved, physiologically. A mirror image of this memory is also preserved by the human spirit so that the compositeness of who you are goes into eternity. That is how you will be known as you were known.

In that day when you have a glorified body, guess what you get back? You get a brand new, entire, physical body including brain cells, that 1 Corinthians 15:53 may be fulfilled, "That corruption shall put on incorruption, and mortality shall put on immortality." You will have a new house to live in and a new brain to house everything you are spiritually. Do you see how that works? It is the only thing that makes any sense.

If you are going to just put your faith in your soul, you have had it. It goes back to dust. I am not going to rely on the physiological part of my physical existence; it is faulty. God does not live in my soul. My soul rejoices in Him, but God the Holy Spirit lives in my spirit man. The real you is a spirit.

My spirit man became born again, and out of that my soul shall be saved and preserved as who I am forever.

That is why you need to pay attention to who you are now. Do not let the devil steal your crown. Do not let the devil lie to you. Do not let the devil become part of your personality.

When I am in sin, God still loves me. His love is constant. He is married to us even if we are backsliding. Remember what Jeremiah said.

> **Turn, O backsliding children, saith the Lord; for I am married unto you: and I will take you one of a city, and two of a family, and I will bring you to Zion:** Jeremiah 3:14

God married a spiritual harlot and made her His wife. I do not know where you are, but I am a spiritual harlot that God loved and betrothed to Jesus from the foundation of the world.

> **According as he hath chosen us in him before the foundation of the world, that we should be holy and without blame before him in love:**
> Ephesians 4:1

In order for you to be free, you must come to that place of understanding where you no longer struggle with yourself, but you make the enemy and his kingdom the problem.

> **For we wrestle not against flesh and blood, but against principalities, against powers, against the rulers of the darkness of this world, against spiritual wickedness in high places.** Ephesians 6:12

I reserve the right to change. Even if the change has not occurred, I refuse to be condemned concerning parts of me that are not right. I refuse to get off my seat in heavenly places and be stereotyped. Let God speak to you and mold you into who you really are.